T0145020

The True Story of Eddie the Duck

WestBow Press books may be ordered through booksellers or by contacting:

WestBow Press
A Division of Thomas Nelson & Zondervan
1663 Liberty Drive
Bloomington, IN 47403
www.westbowpress.com
1 (866) 928-1240

ISBN: 978-1-9736-3971-8 (sc)
ISBN: 978-1-9736-3972-5 (e)

Library of Congress Control Number: 2018910984

Print information available on the last page.

WestBow Press rev. date: 09/17/2018

WestBow
PRESS®
A DIVISION OF THOMAS NELSON
& ZONDERVAN

The True Story of Eddie the Duck

Dee Ashley

It was a bright, beautiful Saturday morning. Ten year old Kelsey loved to wander the farm, exploring all of the places that winter had once hidden. Kelsey had a love for all animals and spring was a perfect time to search for signs of new life.

Suddenly a ray of sunshine fell upon a beautiful sight. Nestled in a soft home of dry leaves was a big blue duck egg. Kelsey had seen duck eggs before. She knew there were many kinds of ducks like wood ducks, mallards, pintails and teal. She also knew that disturbing the egg would discourage the mother duck from returning to her nest.

All day Kelsey watched from a distance to make sure that the duck egg was safe from other animals. Maybe the Mother Duck had returned to her nest. That would have been perfect.

When at last the sun was near setting and the warmth of the April sun gave way to cooler temperatures, Kelsey gently rescued the big, blue egg. Tucking the egg lovingly in a bucket lined with dry leaves, she carried it proudly to the house.

For the rest of the weekend, Kelsey pondered the plan that just might be the key to successfully hatching the big, blue egg. She remembered being in first grade and the excitement of hatching baby chicks.

On Monday morning, her bucket in hand, Kelsey climbed aboard the big, yellow school bus. Her friends on the bus were all curious about the contents of the bucket. They, too, were hoping that someday the egg would hatch.

First Graders had, the week before, carefully placed the chick eggs in the incubator. An incubator is a warm place that would protect them so they could hatch in 21 days. Although a bit unsure of being able to hatch the duck egg, the teacher allowed Kelsey to make room in the incubator for her big, blue duck egg.

Now the wait began. After reading all about duck eggs, Kelsey knew that it would take 28 days for the duck egg to hatch. Excitement grew as they got closer to the 21 days that it would take for the chicks to hatch. Finally the children could hear the cheeeep sounding within the eggs as the tiny chicks hatched out one at a time.

Soon all the chicks were free of their thick, protective shell and they were part of this big, new wonderful world. All except, the big, blue egg that seemed to just sit there, never moving, never cheeping.

As the days past, Kelsey thought maybe her duck egg would never hatch. Each day, she checked on the egg and each day, she left the first grade room with less hope of having her duck egg hatch. After all, the school year would soon come to an end. Then what?

But on a Friday afternoon, just a few days before school was out, a welcome sound came from the big, blue egg. CHEEEEEEP, CHEEEEEEEP it squeaked as it began to rock and roll. First one little hole appeared in the egg then another, then a craaaaaack! But Kelsey knew that the baby inside needed to come out on its own. Sadly, Kelsey, the teacher and the students left for the weekend. What might they find in the incubator when they returned on Monday?

On Saturday morning the teacher returned to her classroom to clean the incubator and view whatever she might find there. As she opened the door to the classroom, she was astounded to hear the loud CHEEEEEP of the most beautiful, tiny mallard duckling.

As the teacher reached in to pick up the baby, the little fellow immediately started pecking on her ring. This is called imprinting. When a duckling is newly born, the first thing he sees, in his mind, is his mother. He thought the teacher's ring was his mother!!

Soon the teacher and the tiny duckling were on their way home. All weekend the duck was the center of attention. When the teacher went for a walk, the little duckling would follow behind his "mother." When the grandchildren came to visit, they fell in love with him, insisting that his name should be Eddie, so Eddie it was. The teacher's husband even brought home a forty pound bag of feed just for their new-found friend.

On Sunday morning, the duckling was the subject of the children's story. The children listened intently as they learned about Eddie, who was very persistent. Even when he was alone in the incubator, he never gave up. They were encouraged to never give up when they were learning to do something new, like riding their bike or learning to read.

When the teacher and Eddie returned to school on Monday, the children were all so happy to see the incubator replaced with Eddie and a cozy nest. Kelsey could hardly wait to claim her latest farm animal friend. As she boarded the bus for home, children happily shouted, Edd….ie, Edd….ie!!!

Now you might think this was the end of the story, but wait_____there's more.

In August, the Woodbury County Fair was in town and it seemed that everyone loved the fair. As the teacher entered the fairgrounds, she heard a familiar voice calling her name from the crowds of people. It was Kelsey, anxiously waiting to show off her surprise. Hand in hand, Kelsey and the teacher headed for the poultry barn. As they came near the duck entries, the teacher couldn't believe her eyes.

There, sporting a big, blue ribbon on the side of his cage was Eddie. He was the most beautiful, full grown mallard duck you've ever seen. When the teacher reached in the cage to pet Eddie, he enthusiastically started pecking on her ring, a sure sign that Eddie had once more found his mother.

Kelsey reported that Eddie ruled the duck pond. Whenever a new duck joined the flock, Eddie gently protected them under his loving wing.

Dedicated to Mrs. Choquette, her colleague, who shared her knowledge about hatching eggs with Mrs. Ashley and to Kelsey Sands who never gave up on Eddie.

A huge "Thank You" to Art Ashley for all of his support in the process of writing this book and to Kim Bata, Brenda Ashley, Shelly Nash, Susie Chesley, Joy Lillie and Allison Crichton for helping to make it happen.

Printed in the United States
By Bookmasters